TOOLS OF THE TRADE

SandCastle
Tools of the Trade

DRILLS

ANDERS HANSON

Consulting Editor, Diane Craig, M.A./Reading Specialist

ABDO
Publishing Company

Published by ABDO Publishing Company, 8000 West 78th Street, Edina, Minnesota 55439.

Printed in the United States.

Editor: Pam Price
Content Developer: Nancy Tuminelly
Cover and Interior Design and Production: Mighty Media
Photo Credits: JupiterImages Corporation, Shutterstock, Palmer, Alfred T.

Library of Congress Cataloging-in-Publication Data
Hanson, Anders, 1980-
  Drills / Anders Hanson.
      p. cm. -- (Tools of the trade)
  ISBN 978-1-60453-581-5
  1. Drilling and boring machinery--Juvenile literature. I. Title.

TJ1263.H35 2009
621.9'52--dc22

                                2008055051

SandCastle™ Level: Fluent

SandCastle™ books are created by a team of professional educators, reading specialists, and content developers around five essential components—phonemic awareness, phonics, vocabulary, text comprehension, and fluency—to assist young readers as they develop reading skills and strategies and increase their general knowledge. All books are written, reviewed, and leveled for guided reading, early reading intervention, and Accelerated Reader® programs for use in shared, guided, and independent reading and writing activities to support a balanced approach to literacy instruction. The SandCastle™ series has four levels that correspond to early literacy development. The levels are provided to help teachers and parents select appropriate books for young readers.

Emerging Readers
(no flags)

Beginning Readers
(1 flag)

Transitional Readers
(2 flags)

Fluent Readers
(3 flags)

SandCastle™ would like to hear from you. Please send us your comments and suggestions.
sandcastle@abdopublishing.com

CONTENTS

What Is a Drill? 4

History 5

Brace **6**

Pistol-Grip Drill **10**

Right-Angle Drill **14**

Hammer Drill **18**

Match Game 22

Tool Quiz 23

Glossary 24

pistol-grip drill

WHAT IS A DRILL?

drill bit

drill

A drill is a tool that cuts holes. A drill has a sharp **spiral** blade called a bit. The drill spins the bit. When a person presses the drill into something, the spinning bit creates a hole.

HISTORY

The oldest known drill is the bow drill. Bow drills are about 7,000 years old. They were used to make fires and drill holes.

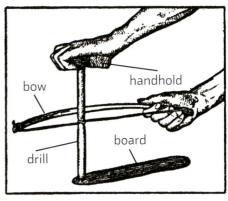

bow
handhold
board
drill

Moving the bow back and forth spins the drill into the board.

hand drill

Hand drills were popular during the seventeenth century.

The electric drill was invented in Australia in 1889.

electric
pistol-grip
drill

BRACE

Braces are hand tools that drill holes. One hand presses down on the handhold. The other hand turns the U-shaped handle.

Some **anglers** use braces to drill holes in the ice.

A chuck is a device that holds a removable bit. A chuck can hold many different kinds of bits.

bit

chuck

When the handle of the brace turns, the bit creates a hole.

handle

The bit spins into wood.

handhold

Roman is going ice fishing. He uses a brace to make a hole in the ice.

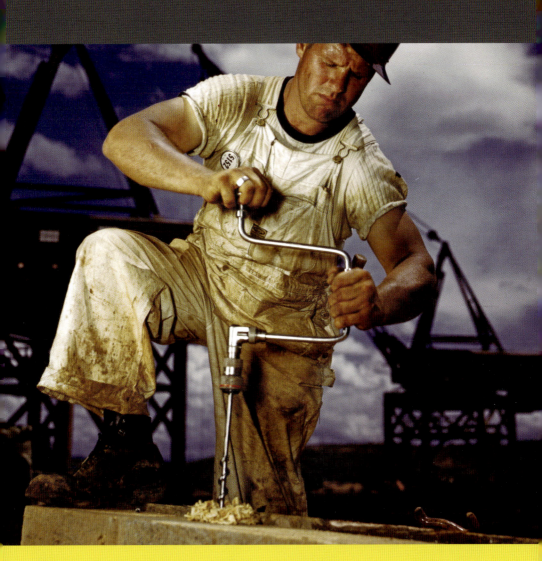

Kevin is a construction worker.
He drills a hole with a brace.

PISTOL-GRIP DRILL

bit   chuck

Pistol-grip drills are very popular. They are **portable** and powerful. Some run on **batteries**. Others have power cords.

different-sized bits

The chuck can hold different types of bits, such as screwdriver bits. Screwdriver bits turn screws.

Pistol-grip drills are powered by electricity.

battery for a cordless drill

direction switch

trigger

The direction switch controls which way the bit spins.

The **trigger** controls how fast the bit turns.

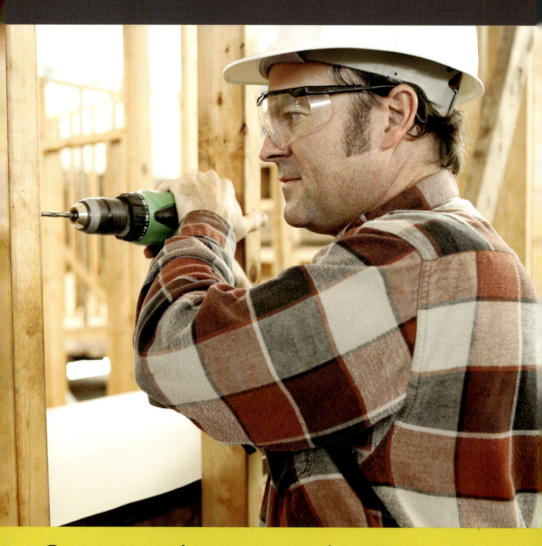

George is working on a new house.
He uses a pistol-grip drill to make a hole.

Albert drills a hole in wood.
He is using a pistol-grip drill.

RIGHT-ANGLE DRILL

chuck

bit

90°

A right angle is a special name for a 90-degree angle. The corners of squares and rectangles are right angles.

Right-angle drills fit into tight spaces.

Plumbers and electricians often use right-angle drills to make holes inside walls.

1132VSR

trigger

Right-angle drills are very powerful, even at low speeds.

Candice needs to drill a hole below a **radiator**. She uses a right-angle drill.

Julio is **installing** the electrical system in a new house. He drills a hole with a right-angle drill.

HAMMER DRILL

bit

chuck

switch

handle

A hammer drill is part hammer, part drill. Like other drills, a hammer drill turns the drill bit. But a hammer drill also moves the bit back and forth. This back and forth motion is called hammering.

Hammer drills have a switch to turn the hammering action on and off. When hammering is off, the drill acts like a pistol-grip drill.

The bit on a hammer drill spins and moves back and forth.

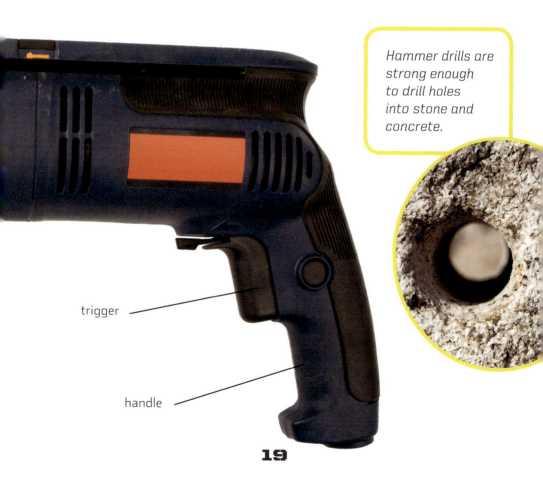

Hammer drills are strong enough to drill holes into stone and concrete.

trigger

handle

Heidi is drilling into concrete.
She uses a hammer drill.

Tammy is fixing up her basement. She uses a hammer drill to make a hole in the brick.

MATCH GAME

Match the words to the pictures! The answers are on the bottom of the page.

1. hammer drill

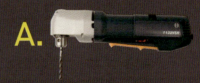

A.

2. brace

B.

3. right-angle drill

C.

4. pistol-grip drill

D.

Answers: 1)D 2)B 3)A 4)C

22

TOOL QUIZ

Test your tool knowledge with this quiz!
The answers are on the bottom of the page.

1. A brace is a hand tool.
   True or false?

2. Pistol-grip drills are powered by electricity. True or false?

3. Right-angle drills are too big to fit into tight spaces. True or false?

4. Hammer drills can move a bit back and forth. True or false?

GLOSSARY

angler – someone who fishes with a hook.

battery – a device that changes chemical energy into electricity.

install – to place or fasten something so that it can be used.

plumber – a person who installs and repairs pipes.

portable – easily moved or carried.

radiator – a device that gives off heat.

spiral – winding around a central axis.

trigger – a small device that causes something to happen when pressed.

To see a complete list of SandCastle™ books and other nonfiction titles from ABDO Publishing Company, visit www.abdopublishing.com.
8000 West 78th Street, Edina, MN 55439 • 800-800-1312 • fax 952-831-1632